Alex

and the

Elephant

Karin Ahrenholz

Balboa Press books may be ordered through booksellers or by contacting:

Balboa Press
A Division of Hay House
1663 Liberty Drive
Bloomington, IN 47403
www.balboapress.com
1 (877) 407-4847

ISBN: 978-1-5043-4581-1 (sc)
ISBN: 978-1-5043-4582-8 (e)

Print information available on the last page.

Balboa Press rev. date: 11/24/2015

BALBOA
PRESS
A DIVISION OF HAY HOUSE

Alex

and the

Elephant

Karin Ahrenholz

Once upon a time, there was a little boy named Alex. His Grandma and Grandpa had just given him a book about zoo animals. That night, Alex's mother read it to him. As she read the book, Alex liked all of the animals, but his favorite was the Elephant. He thought it was neat the way they used their trunks to do everything.

After his mother finished reading the book, Alex asked her if they could go to the zoo. She said maybe they could go tomorrow. Then she told him to dream about the animals as she closed the door.

When Alex woke up the next morning, he jumped out of bed and ran to the kitchen where his mother was cooking breakfast. She said "Good morning" and Alex quickly asked her if they could go to the zoo. His mother said, "Yes." Alex was so excited that he could barely eat his breakfast.

When they got to the Zoo, they bought the tickets and went in. It was a beautiful day and Alex was very excited to see the Elephants.

He had never before seen so many animals. They saw monkeys, parrots, bears, lions, tigers, ducks and zebras, but no elephants.

They were almost at the back of the zoo when Alex saw a sign for the Elephant Exhibit. He tugged on his mother's arm so she could see it too. The sign pointed to just around the next corner.

When they got there, they heard a strange sound. Alex let go of his mother's arm and ran over to a gate where the noise was coming from.

There, a baby elephant had gotten his ear caught when the zookeeper closed the gate. Alex shook the gate and the baby elephant was able to pull his ear out.

But when he freed himself, he hurt his ear. There was a triangle shape cut out of his ear.

Other than that, he was fine. Alex's mother ran over to see what was happening.

Alex told her how he freed the baby elephant from being caught in the gate. His mother told him that he was very brave. Then she said the words that Alex would never forget. "If you do a favor for someone, that favor will one day be returned to you." The mother elephant walked over to Alex and his mother and looked at them as if she was saying "Thank you." Then she went over to comfort her baby.

On the way home, Alex thought about what happened at the zoo. He also thought about what his mother had said to him, about how that favor would one day be returned to him. Alex wondered how an elephant could ever return a favor.

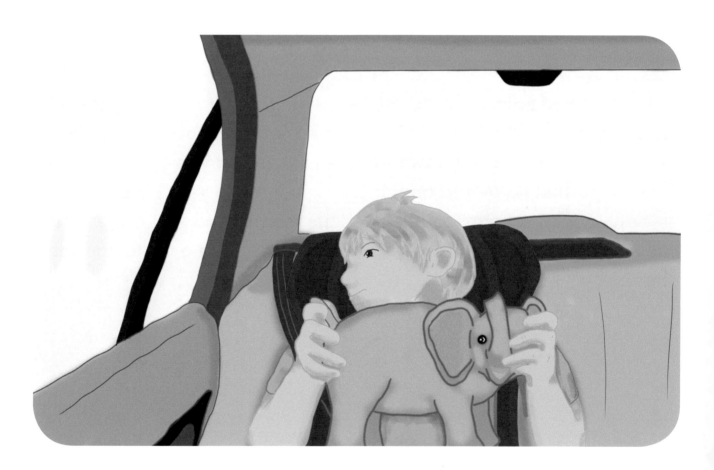

As the years passed, Alex eventually got married and had a child of his own. A little girl named Lauren.

When Lauren was three years old, Alex took her to the zoo. They saw many different animals and Lauren was having a wonderful time.

They finally made their way back to the Elephant Exhibit. Lauren was so little that she could not see the elephants behind the wall. Alex held her up on the top of the wall so she was able to see them.

Lauren was so excited that she wriggled right out of Alex's hands and fell into the elephant exhibit! Alex couldn't reach her.

Suddenly, one of the big elephants started walking towards Lauren. She was too scared to move. Alex didn't know what to do. With eyes wide open, he took a deep breath. Just then, a wonderful thing happened!

The elephant put its trunk down on the ground and slid it under Lauren's body. Then it wrapped it around her, lifted her into the air and put her back onto the wall. Alex reached out for Lauren and grabbed her. The Elephant had saved Lauren!

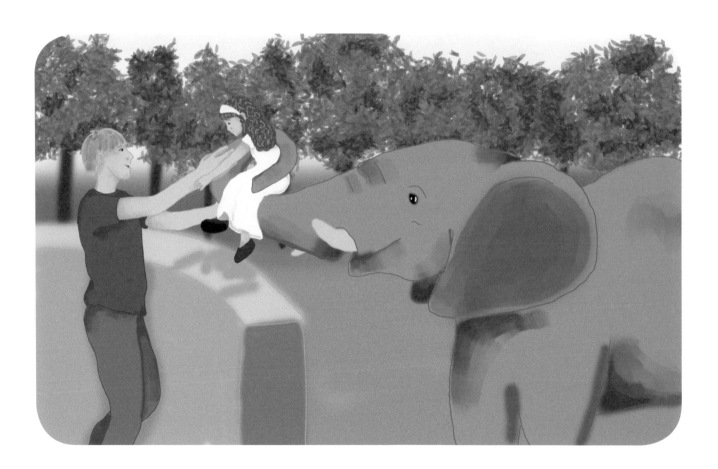

Alex gave Lauren a big hug and as he did, he looked at the elephant who was looking back at him. Alex noticed the elephant's ear had the shape of a triangle cut out of it. It was the same elephant he had saved when he was a boy!

Alex thought about the words his mother had told him. The words he never forgot. "If you do a favor for someone, that favor will one day be returned to you." The words were true. The elephant had returned the favor from many years ago.

As they both stood and looked at each other, neither one of them ever forgot what happened to them on that day. Nor will they ever forget what happened to them on this day. The day the elephant got to truly thank Alex by returning his favor.

THE END

Printed in the United States
by Baker & Taylor Publisher Services